COOL MACHINES

TEN TRACTORS and FARM MACHINES

JP Percy

D1423525
C016692401

Franklin Watts
First published in Great Britain in 2017 by The Watts Publishing Group
Copyright © The Watts Publishing Group 2017

Credits
Series Editor: Amy Pimperton
Series Designer: Mo Choy Design Ltd.
Picture Researcher: Diana Morris
Picture credits: aoo3771/Shutterstock: front cover tl. Bluetoes67/Dreamstime: 17b, 18, 27tr. Casadaphoto/
Shutterstock: 17t. Stephen Clarke/Shutterstock: 5. Perry Correll/Shutterstock: 15t. Desha & Cam/Shutterstock:
front cover cl. Duzunov/Shutterstock: front cover cr. Tom Fawls/Wikimedia Commons: 15c. Fotokostic/
Shutterstock: front cover tc. JCB: 22, 23c, 27cr, 29t. Katatonia82/Dreamstime: 21b Kvernland: 10, 11t, 11b, 26cr.
Logset: 24, 25t, 25b, 27bl, 31t. Lucid Waters/Dreamstime: 21t. New Holland: 16, 27tl. Orientaly/Shutterstock: front
cover br. Sergiy Palamarchuk /Dreamstime: 19c. Rootstock/Shutterstock: 7t. Federico Rostanno/Shutterstock:
front cover tr. Seed hawker.com: 12, 13t, 13b, 26cl. Smereka/Shutterstock: front cover c, club, bl; 23t. Taina
Sohlman/Dreamstime: 7b. Taina Sohlman/Shutterstock: 4, 6, 26tr, 30. Soldem2/Dreamstime: 14, 26br. Stefan
II/Dreamstime: front cover main, 1. Tanger/Shutterstock: front cover bc. traktorpool.de: 9b. Fabio de Villa/
Shutterstock: 8, 26tl. Jim West/Alamy: 9t. Wikimedia Commons: 19t. © Yamaha Motors: 2t, 20, 27cl, 31b.
Every attempt has been made to clear copyright. Should there be any
inadvertent omission please apply to the publisher for rectification.

HB ISBN   978 1 4451 5514 2
PB ISBN   978 1 4451 5515 9

Printed in China

Franklin Watts
An imprint of
Hachette Children's Group
Part of The Watts Publishing Group
Carmelite House
50 Victoria Embankment
London EC4Y 0DZ

An Hachette UK Company
www.hachette.co.uk
www.franklinwatts.co.uk

Note to parents and teachers: Every effort has been made by the Publishers to ensure that the websites in
this book are suitable for children, that they are of the highest educational value, and that they contain
no inappropriate or offensive material. However, because of the nature of the Internet, it is impossible to
guarantee that the contents of these sites will not be altered. We strongly advise that Internet access is
supervised by a responsible adult.

CONTENTS

Words in **bold** can be found in the glossary on pages 30–31.

COOL FARM MACHINES!

Here are ten of the coolest farm machines you'll ever see! But they're not just amazing to look at. They're cool because they are useful, powerful and tough enough to do all the hard work on a farm.

Tractor – go to pages 6–7.

Farm vehicles do all sorts of different jobs. Tractors and quad bikes are used for lots of tasks and can zip around on roads and in fields. Other farm machines do special jobs — spreading **fertiliser** or making hay **bales**. Without them, farmers would find it hard to grow **crops** and look after their animals.

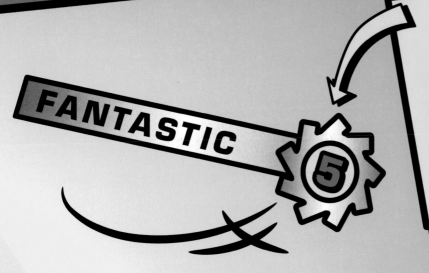

FANTASTIC 5

Look out for the Fantastic 5 panels. Here you'll find out five fantastic facts about each vehicle.

Combine harvester – go to pages 16–17.

BUSY

A TRACTOR is the most important vehicle a farmer can own. They have to be strong and sturdy, but nippy enough to whizz about the farm. These busy machines never stop.

Huge wheels, a powerful engine and a chunky body make light work of the toughest tasks. This *NEW HOLLAND T7.250* is an **all-purpose** tractor. Special **adaptors** mean it can pull trailers or other machines that **sow** crops or move heavy things, such as hay bales, out of the way.

TOUGH
The four, big, chunky tyres have a thick tread on them. This helps the tractor drive over rough and muddy ground without getting stuck.

BRIGHT
Tractors often work at night, too. Powerful lights are useful when farmers have to work in the fields after dark.

FANTASTIC

5

NEW HOLLAND T7.250

- **Length:** 5.7 metres
- **Weight:** 7.3 tonnes
- **Maximum speed:** 50 kilometres per hour
- **Height:** 3.1 metres
- **Engine power:** 250 **horsepower**

MUCKY

Sometimes work on a farm can be very mucky! Some farmers use animal poo – called manure – to fertilise the soil. They spread the manure using a MANURE SPREADER.

Poo from animals, such as cows, has stuff in it that helps crops to grow bigger and better. Small manure spreaders spray smelly manure out of the back of the machine, covering the soil with a layer of poo! Giant machines like this *VEENHUIS EUROJECT 3500* **inject** the manure straight into the soil.

SELL IT ON

Liquid manure is called slurry. Dairy (cow) farmers often collect up slurry, store it and then sell it to other farmers.

VEENHUIS EUROJECT 3500

- ⚙ **Maximum width:** 8.7 metres
- ⚙ **Number of hoses:** 30
- ⚙ **Weight:** 3.6 tonnes
- ⚙ **Number of injectors:** 72–100
- ⚙ **Tank capacity:** Up to 36,000 litres

TUCKED IN

The hoses fold up and out of the way as the manure spreader and tank are pulled by tractor from farmyard to field.

SLICING

PLOUGHS do very important work on the farm. They turn the soil in a field over and make the long lines that crops are sown in.

Farms are busy places with lots of jobs that need doing. Modern ploughs can prepare a huge field for sowing in no time. The *KVERNLAND PW RW's* steel blades are **heat-treated** with fire when they are made. This makes the metal extra-tough so it can slice easily through heavy or stony soil.

LINE UP
The long lines a plough makes are called furrows. Neat lines of crops are faster and easier to harvest in the autumn.

CUT IN
To make each furrow, a blade cuts into the soil and flips the earth to one side.

FANTASTIC 5

KVERNLAND PW RW

⚙ **Length:** 2 metres

⚙ **Weight:** 7.6 tonnes

⚙ **Engine power:** 360 horsepower

⚙ **Number of blades:** 7–14

⚙ **Furrow width:** 35-50 cm

DRILLING

Farmers used to plant seeds by hand. Today they use giant SEED DRILLS to plant thousands of seeds in a single day.

The seeds are towed behind the tractor in a **hopper**, such as the *980 AIR CART*. Jets of air blast the seeds along tubes to the *SEED HAWK XL TOOLBAR*. Each seed is drilled down into the soil by the toolbar, which helps stop mice and birds eating the seeds before they can grow into crops.

SEED HAWK XL TOOLBAR AND *980 AIR CART*

- ⚙ **Toolbar width:** 25 metres
- ⚙ **Number of seed rows:** 84
- ⚙ **Air cart length:** 14.5 metres
- ⚙ **Air cart height:** 5 metres
- ⚙ **Air cart capacity:** 35,640 litres

NEAT KNIFE
Next to each seed drill is a fertiliser knife. This makes a hole in the soil next to the seed, so that any fertiliser spread on the soil gets as close to the seed as possible.

AIR POWER
When a machine, such as an air cart, uses jets of gas to power things along, it is said to work pneumatically. The gas is under huge pressure, which gives it its power.

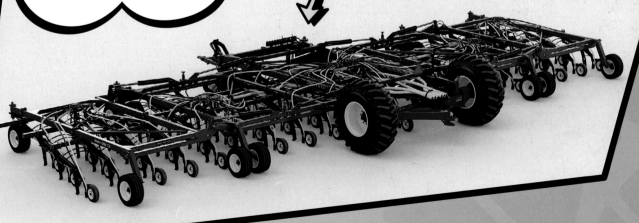

SWOOPING

Small CROP-DUSTING AIRCRAFT or air tractors swoop down low over fields to release their load of fertiliser to help crops grow. Or they release **pesticides** to kill pests, such as plant-eating bugs.

For very large fields, often in **remote** places, farmers hire pilots to fly planes low over their fields to perform crop dusting. The *AIR TRACTOR AT-502B* makes tight twists and turns as it zooms from one end of the field to the other, spraying the crops as it flies.

SPRAY OUT
Nozzles under the wings spray a fine mist of fertiliser or pesticides over the crops.

SPIN AROUND
The nozzles are fed by a pump that is powered by a small **propeller** under the belly of the plane. The propeller whizzes around as the plane flies.

FANTASTIC 5

AIR TRACTOR AT-502B

⚙ **Wing span:** 15.8 metres

⚙ **Cruising speed:** 250 kilometres per hour

⚙ **Spraying speed:** 195–230 kilometres per hour

⚙ **Spraying tank:** 1,893 litres

⚙ **Engine type:** 2,200 **rpm** propeller

WIDE

One of the biggest machines on a farm is a COMBINE HARVESTER. They sweep through fields of crops, harvesting huge amounts of grain at a time.

The widest part of a combine harvester is called the head. Farmers can take off and put on different types of head to harvest different grains, such as wheat or rice. A *NEW HOLLAND CR10.90* holds the world record for the most wheat harvested in eight hours – 797 tonnes!

FANTASTIC **5**

NEW HOLLAND CR10.90

⚙ **Weight:** 25 tonnes

⚙ **Engine power:** 653 horsepower

⚙ **Grain tank:** 14,500 litres

⚙ **Head width:** 13.7 metres

⚙ **Top speed:** 40 kph

SHOOT OUT

The grains are separated from the stalks inside the machine. The grain then shoots out of a pipe, called an unloader, into the back of a waiting truck.

SPREAD A LOAD

Some of the biggest combine harvesters have **caterpillar tracks** over the wheels. They help spread the weight of this heavy machine to stop it sinking into the ground.

SQUASHED

Hay bales are really useful on a farm. Straw or grass is squashed into a round or rectangular shape by a HAY BALER and stored to feed farm animals in the winter.

Hay balers are towed behind a tractor. They rake up the straw into a huge container, chop it and then squash it into a hay bale shape. Then it rolls out of the back of the machine covered in netting. Neat! The bales can be small or large. The *LELY WELGER RP545* makes some of the biggest bales around.

TINY TINES

The thin, metal rakes that pick up the hay are called tines. They spin very fast on a wheel at the front of the machine.

SILAGE

Some bales are wrapped in plastic. Inside, the hay or grass **ferments** to turn into **silage**, which farm animals eat in the winter.

FANTASTIC

5

LELY WELGER RP545

- **Length:** 5.2 metres
- **Width:** 2.7 metres
- **Weight:** 5 tonnes
- **Bale size:** 1–2 metres diameter
- **Engine power:** 120 horsepower

NIPPY

Farmers love a QUAD BIKE for speeding around on the farm. These cool ATV machines can get to places bigger vehicles simply can't reach. ATV stands for All Terrain Vehicle.

Farmers use quad bikes to do all sorts of jobs. The *YAMAHA GRIZZLY 700 ATV* can tow a trailer, splash with ease through muddy ground, bring food to animals in remote places and zip along narrow tracks among the trees. In an emergency, these speedy machines can take a farmer quickly from farmyard to field to help injured or sick animals.

FANTASTIC

ROUND UP
It's not just sheepdogs that are good at herding animals. ATVs are perfect for rounding up sheep and cows on steep hillsides.

YAMAHA GRIZZLY 700 ATV

⚙ **Length:** 2 metres

⚙ **Width:** 1.2 metres

⚙ **Top speed:** 110 kph

⚙ **Towing power:** 600 kilogrammes

⚙ **Colours:** 7 (including a cool camouflage one)

RACING
ATV's are a lot of fun too. Lots of farmers let ATV racing happen on their land. People compete over a rough course to see who can make it round the fastest!

HANDY

Sometimes farmers need a machine that can do lots of things. A TELEHANDLER is a handy bit of kit that can lift, move, stack, push and tow.

A *JCB 560-80 AGRI* can easily switch between jobs on the farm. The front end of the **boom** can be used with lots of different attachments. Large buckets scoop up grain or animal feed. Forks spear hay bales and stack them up and shovels can push piles of stuff, such as manure around the farmyard.

⑤

STRETCH OUT

The word, 'telehandler', is short for 'telescopic handler'. This means the boom extends, like a telescope, to reach high into the air.

FANTASTIC

JCB 560-80 AGRI

⚙ **Engine power:** 145 horsepower

⚙ **Weight:** 11 tonnes

⚙ **Lifting power:** 6 tonnes

⚙ **Maximum boom height:** 8 metres

⚙ **Maximum speed:** 40 kph

GRAB IT!

Special attachments with claws, called power grabs, are used to move objects, such as huge tree trunks, out of the way. The forks close around the object, like a cage.

MONSTER

HARVESTERS work in thick forests, chopping down massive trees so that they can be turned into timber and paper products.

The monster *LOGSET 12H GTE* is one of the biggest harvesters in the world. It makes short work of chopping down trees. Its harvester head clamps around the tree trunk and its chainsaw slices through it. Then the strong boom lifts the tree up as the trunk is sliced into sections, all in just a few seconds.

FANTASTIC

LOGSET 12H GTE

- ⚙ **Weight:** 24.5 tonnes
- ⚙ **Length:** 9 metres
- ⚙ **Engine power:** 300 horsepower
- ⚙ **Electric motor power:** 240 horsepower
- ⚙ **Boom length:** 11 metres

TWO BOGIES

The body of the machine has two sections joined together, called bogies. Each bogie has four wheels. The driver's **cab** sits in the middle between the two.

CHOP AND STRIP

As the trunk slides through the harvester head and is chopped into pieces, sharp knives slice off any branches. A debarker strips bark from the trunk.

TEN MORE COOL FACTS

BUSY: The first tractors were powered by steam engines. The **NEW HOLLAND T7.250** has a modern diesel engine.

MUCKY: The slurry in the **VEENHUIS EUROJECT 3500's** tank is smelly because it has methane in it – a type of natural gas.

SLICING: The **KVERNLAND PW RW** plough has lots of springs on it. The springs help the plough bounce over large rocks so it won't get stuck.

DRILLING: The **SEED HAWK XL TOOLBAR** can sow up to 125 kilogrammes of seed in every 4,000 square metres. That's a lot of seeds!

SWOOPING: The **AIR TRACTOR AT-502B** is used most often on remote farms with lots of very large fields, such as in North America and Australia.

WIDE: The **NEW HOLLAND CR10.90** can harvest up to 135 tonnes of grain in just one hour!

SQUASHED: The hay bales that the **LELY WELGER RP545** make can weigh up to 600 kilogrammes.

NIPPY: Another name for an ATV, such as the **YAMAHA GRIZZLY 700**, is 'quad bike'. This name comes from the fact it has four wheels, but you ride it a bit like a bike.

HANDY: The **JCB 560-80 AGRI** can have roof guards fitted to it. These metal bars stop heavy objects crushing the driver's cab if they fall on it.

MONSTER: The driver's cab in the **LOGSET 12H GTE** can spin around in a full circle, so the driver can see all around.

STACK UP THOSE STATS!

Here are the ten cool machines with all their stats and a few more. Which is your favourite?

	NEW HOLLAND T7.250	VEENHUIS Euroject 3500	KVERNLAND PW RW	980 AIR CART	AIR TRACTOR AT-502B
Weight	7.3 tonnes	3.6 tonnes	7.6 tonnes		4 tonnes
Height	3.1 metres		80 centimetres	5 metres	3.5 metres
Length	5.7 metres		2 metres	15 metres	10 metres
Top speed	50 kph				250 kph
Width	2.5 metres	8.7 metres	6 metres	5–6 metres	15.8 metres
Engine type	Diesel				2,200 rpm propeller
Engine power	250 hp		360 hp		750 hp
Tank capacity		36,000 litres		35,640 litres	1,893 litres
Wheel size	1 metre			1 metre	25 centimetres
Number of wheels	4	2–8		6	2
Boom					

Air Tractor AT-502B is the fastest machine

QUIZ

1 Why do some tractors have powerful lights?

2 What is manure made of?

3 How can a plough's blades be made extra-tough?

4 How wide is the Seed Hawk toolbar?

5 What is another name for a crop-dusting aircraft?

New Holland CR10.90 is the heaviest machine

NEW HOLLAND CR10.90	LELY WELGER RP545	YAMAHA GRIZZLY 700 ATV	JCB 560-80 AGRI	LOGSET 12H GTE
25 tonnes	5 tonnes		11 tonnes	24.5 tonnes
4 metres	3 metres	1.2 metres	3 metres	4 metres
9 metres	5.2 metres	2 metres	5 metres	9 metres
40 kph		110 kph	40 kph	
13.7 metres (Head width)	2.7 metres	1.2 metres	2.5 metres	3 metres
Biodiesel		Petrol	Diesel	Diesel
653 hp	120 hp	45 hp	145 hp	300 hp
14,500 litres				
		66 centimetres	60 centimetres	70 centimetres
	2		4	8
			8 metres	11 metres

Logset 12H GTE has the most wheels

kph = kilometres per hour   lpm = litres per minute   hp = horsepower

6 What type of crop does a combine harvester collect?

7 What is hay used for?

8 What can an ATV do that a sheepdog can do, too?

9 How much weight can a JCB 560-80 AGRI lift?

10 What is a machine that fells trees called?

GLOSSARY

adaptor something that connects one thing to another

all-purpose something that can do lots of different jobs, instead of one special job

bale a large bundle or package that is tightly packed and tied together

boom the long arm on a machine, used for lifting

cab the separate front part of a large vehicle, where the driver sits

capacity space inside an engine

caterpillar tracks a belt of plates that goes around the wheels of a vehicle to help it move and stop it sinking into soft ground

crops plants that are grown on a farm and sold

fertiliser a natural or human-made material that is sprayed over crops to make them grow faster and stronger

ferment when a crop goes through a chemical change which means it can be kept for longer

grain a small, hard seed, such as wheat or rice

harvest cutting down and collecting crops

heat-treated when metal is heated up and cooled down to make it even stronger

hopper a box with a hole in the bottom that grain is slowly fed through

Further Information

WEBSITES:

https://www.deere.com/en/connect-with-john-deere/john-deere-for-kids/

Visit the John Deere children's website to find out all about farm machines. You can also watch videos of farm machines in action, play grames and read farmyard stories, featuring characters like Corey Combine.

http://www.virtualfarmwalk.org/visit.html

Take a virtual walk around a farm! This website lets you explore life down on the farm and includes sections on farm machines, animals and what happens to farm food when it is sold. It also has a section of fun activity sheets to help you get the most out of your visit.

BOOKS

Machines at Work: Tractors by Clive Gifford (Wayland)

Mechanic Mike's Machines: Farm Machines by David West (Franklin Watts)

Working Wheels: Tractor by Annabel Savery (Franklin Watts)

PLACES TO VISIT

There are farms you can visit all over the UK. Have a look at the LEAF website to find one near you.

horsepower a unit that shows how powerful an engine is

inject to force a liquid into something

pesticides a natural or human-made material that kills bugs and other minibeasts

propeller a set of spinning blades that push air or liquids along

remote far away from where most people live

RPM stands for Revolutions Per Minute; a way of measuring how fast something spins around

silage grass or grain that has been stored, which is then fed to farm animals during the winter

sow planting seeds

terrain rough ground

INDEX

QUIZ ANSWERS

1 Some tractors have bright lights so that they can work in fields at night.

2 Manure is made of poo from farm animals, such as cows.

3 Some plough blades are heat-treated in fire, which makes the metal super-strong.

4 The Seed Hawk toolbar is 25 metres wide.

5 A crop-dusting aircraft is also called an air tractor.

6 Combine harvesters collect grains, such as wheat or rice.

7 Hay is used to feed animals in the winter.

8 An ATV can be used to herd sheep.

9 A JCB 580-60 AGRI can lift six tonnes.

10 A machine that fells trees is called a harvester.